MW00629751

For permission requests, write to the publisher, addressed "Attention:
Permissions Coordinator," at the address below.

Harmony Close,
Kewtown,
Providenciales
Turks & Caicos Islands

ISBN: 9781916296756

https://cyrildorsiepublish.wixsite.com/website

THE PAIN WAS FOR MY GAIN

TABLE OF CONTENTS

Holy Spirit I pray for the individuals or whomsoever is reading this book to be blessed and that their understanding is enlightened, hope restored and every feeling of illusion be put to shame through the blood of Jesus.

Amen.

4

CHAPTER 1
Introduction

Chapter One

From a very early age, I knew that something was different, and eventually this peculiarity had to be discovered. Like many others, you wonder about your reason and purpose in this world. I guess many of us at some point and time have had these thoughts in our minds and for me, this has been no exception.

As a child growing up I just knew something was unique about me but what it was- I didn't know. But like everything going on in our lives time always reveals itself to us.

It amazes us how quickly time passes so that we can hardly keep up with it! It would of course take the Holy Spirit to bring things to our remembrance,past, present and future.

John 14:26 KJV.

But the comforter, which is the Holy Ghost, whom the Father will send in my name, He shall teach you all things, and bring all things to your remembrance, whatsoever I have said unto you.

Holy Spirit, I pause to give you thanks for my past. I am aware that you are able to heal me from yesterday's wounds. Heal the one that is reading right now, help him or her to understand that they cannot change the past, but they can take effect on the future. We thank you, Lord, for your peace in knowing this. Amen

Growing up I have heard words such as "your past is intrinsically linked to your future". Words such as "you can't change your past, but you can take effect on your future".

Yes, of course, whether good or bad, there are multiple lessons we have learned and most of it has helped us to mature along life's path. For example, if you haven't gone through that storm you would not have made it to the shoreline, God has a way of allowing our storms to teach us life lessons.

As a child, I have truly encountered a lot of storms from my youth right into adulthood and ongoing. I believe with all my heart that even though many of them were meant to kill me I survived them because God had a plan and purpose that lead us towards our destiny.

Psalms 66:12

Thou didsnt cause men to ride over our heads: we went through fire and through water: But though broughtest us out into a wealthy place.

CHAPTER 2
No Cross No Crown

Chapter Two

Every beauty pageant I have watched in my life had taken some preparation and courage. I believed with all my heart that each contestant had a price to pay but at the end of it, only one walked away with the crown.

Unlike anything, I could never understand the mystery of my suffering. It was deeper than my imagination until I realized that it was our Lord's responsibility to be put before the cross in order to bring about a resurrection.

And said unto them, thus it is written, and thus it behooved Christ to suffer, and to rise from the dead the third day.

Luke 24:46-47 KJV

After carefully searching the scriptures, I understood that our Lord was not reputable.

He was willing to do whatever it took to save us all and if we are not willing to go to the cross we could never obtain the crown.

But made himself of no reputation, and took upon him the form of a servant and was made in the likeness of men.

Philippians 2:7

CHAPTER 3

God Qualifies the Caller

Chapter Three

Insecurities have threatened many of us along life's path, especially after being broken, bruised and battered by whatever means or tools the enemy uses for us.

Loss of hope, weak and blurred vision, I earnestly believe the enemy uses these tools to keep us frustrated, drained and to prevent us from coming into our own purposes.

Whenever our spirits have been worn out by depression, anxiety, and fatigue, we are a candidate for the enemy to sit on, and on top of this, when our visions are blurred, there is no telling of the mistakes that one will make before coming into purpose.

Maybe you are reading this book and like me, the enemy has had you bound for many years. Your hopes, dreams, and aspirations have been shattered! I'm here to tell you, please don't give up the best is yet to come!

CHAPTER 4
The Cage Was Not Meant To Kill You

Chapter Four

Feeling caged is one of the worst experiences any human can ever encounter on Planet Earth. I have convinced myself many times that the type of pain I was feeling was not from God, and that if He loved me He would never have allowed me to go through this cage experience.

But I came to understand, not only did He love me but like the prophet Job, He was boasting about me and pushing me toward my purpose of helping others and especially myself.

Isaiah 37: 3

And they said that's him, thus saith Hezekiah, This day is a day of trouble, and of rebuke, and of blasphemy for the children are come to birth, and there is not strength to bring forth.

It felt for me that the pains of my past would never end, and maybe you that are reading this book felt the same way. Have you ever found yourself in situations where you know if God didn't come through you'd perish? Well for me, I came to the realization that not only did God allow the storm, but He created it so that I could be drawn closer to Him.

The excruciating pain we felt, makes us want to give up and as human beings, it's really normal. But what is never normal is the fact that we cannot control the anger, the fear, and the disappointment that comes with it. It has to be a second man preventing us from becoming victims of suicidal tendencies. This especially becomes frustrating for those of you whom the master our Lord and Saviour have in His hands.

.

Lamentation 3:32 KJV

But though he cause grief, yet will he have compassion according to the multitude of his mercies.

CHAPTER 5

His Grace

Chapter Five

I was now convinced that my pain was connected to His grace. He was that second man that stood beside me, He controlled that which I was unable to handle. He wiped my eyes, when I was unable to, His grace was bigger than my pain!

Like the Apostle Paul when the blind has been removed from our eyes, we realize that our infirmities were a testing of our faith so that God's glory can be placed upon us. Furthermore, it displays how amazing our God is to have brought us through the way of crisis so that we could be able to withstand the struggle of the enemy.

2nd Corinthians 12:9

And he said unto me, my grace is sufficient for thee: For my strength is made perfect in weakness. Most gladly therefore will I rather glory in my infirmities, that the power of Christ may rest upon me.

CHAPTER 6

Time Heals

Chapter Six

No matter how long it takes, God has a way of rewarding his children at the end of the tunnel. His plan and purpose for our life will never be aborted until our destiny has been fulfilled. I have now come to the understanding that our spiritual eyes have to become open if we are going to win the race! Maybe like me, you too would have never thought that your eyes could become open.

I am here to say never give up! When your vision seems blurred, know whose onboard the ship with you. God has made us wonderful promises in His word. We must be willing to wait and watch God fulfil each one. The fire that God had allowed us to pass through was to build character and make us stronger. Whatever the situations are there's light at the end of the tunnel.

Luke 4: 18-19

The spirit of the Lord is upon me because he hath anointed me to preach the Gospel to the poor: he hath send me to heal the broken hearted, to preach.

CHAPTER 7

He Delivers On Time

Chapter Seven

Most times I felt as if God was taking either too long or that He had forgotten about me, and am pretty convinced that you at some time in your life might have felt the same way. The prophet Jeremiah stated, "God knows his plans towards us", even if we can't feel him, He is still there. Frustrated, heartbroken or whatever conditions we might find ourselves in God always has a plan for our lives.

Can I say, the enemy was also aware and because of it he tries to lay seize upon every anointed vessel of God claiming them for his own, but we serve a big God who sees and knows everything and will not allow the enemy to win! Rest assured God promises us hope, and our future is bright!

For I know the plans I have for you declares the Lord; plans to prosper you and not to harm you, plans to give you hope and a future. Jeremiah 29:11

CHAPTER 8

No Pain No Gain

Chapter Eight

Have you ever decided to go for a checkup and discover that as long as you stayed away everything seemed to be fine? As soon as you found out that perhaps cholesterol was a little high or blood pressure seemed unstable the worries just started. This becomes a reality when the devil recognizes that our visions are no longer blurred, the real fight only started when God opened my spiritual eyes.

I realized that where the enemy wanted me I was not destined to be. I now realize I was not fulfilling my purpose and the enemy knew it. Unlike many, I wanted to be sure, and if I am a part of the plan I am in it to win it! You, too, have a purpose, and you must never give up. You, too, have a future and a hope you must come to an expected end.

Hebrews 12: 1-2

Let us lay aside every weight and the sin which doth so easily beset us and let us run with patience the race that is set before us.

The enemy was pretty much aware that my eyes were open. Not only did he bring back my past pain, but he started to speak to my mind. He now recognized that I was coming into the perfect will of God for my life, even though he could never stop it. It was his job to pick a fight making sure I would become frustrated, angry and hoping that I would give up the fight.

One of the things that helped me to fight the good fight of hope was having to endure so much for a long time. I am certain that the God who had kept me in the most trying time of my life, is still the same God. Sometimes it's so easy to forget the power of God when tribulation and trials are at their best, but we must be able to quote the word of God back to the enemy.

When our spiritual eyes are open it is not easy for the enemy to win, but we must never forget who is on board the ship with us. Please be reminded, I personally have gone through many of these instances before, so this becomes nothing new. I now realise that the devil our adversary is coming with no new tricks, but he is simply coming using the same tools but in different ways.

It is amazing to see how the enemy would go the extra mile to destroy us and many times if we don't recognize this, we fall prey to his techniques and schemes. We must be fully equipped if we are going to stay in the race.

Let us lay aside every weight and the sin which doth so easily beset us and let us run with patience the race that is set before us.

Hebrews 12: 1-2

We must always be alert if we are going to stay in the race, like the apostle Paul, we must be fully clothed, and we must understand our wrestle. Many years ago I really likened my wrestle to human beings. I will try my best to explain this. Even though I have had opposition from human individuals that got on my last nerve, I also realized that every time something good was about to happen in my life it is in those times that the enemy would show up in this form. I must admit that I didn't realize this right away because many times I gave in and got the good satisfaction of battling with whomever it was at that time. However, I soon realised that this was pushing me further out of God's presence.

Put on the whole armour of God that ye may be able to stand against the wiles of the devil. For we wrestle not against flesh and blood, but against principalities, against powers, against the rulers of the darkness of this world, against spiritual wickedness in High places.

Ephesians 6:11-12

Where God's presence is, there is liberty and peace, when there is no peace there is no joy when there is no joy, sadness shows his face. This was true for me because I found myself drifting in other directions, emotionally wrecked by the deception of the enemy.

When you truly taste of God this reality becomes even harder. There is a missing link and that link spells your peace. Here I can say separation from God opens up the door to anger, emotional breakdown, dissatisfaction, frustration and so much more. It is never a good feeling.

Thou will keep him in perfect peace, whose mind is stayed on thee- because he trusteth in thee.

Isaiah 26:3

CHAPTER 9

Back on Track

Chapter Nine

God will never allow His anointed ones to stay in conditions that are not conducive. He is married to the backslider, in other words His promise to you and me is to bring us to His expected end. He promises us hope and a future.

He will not change his mind, but we must be able to understand our wrestle and our fight is not with flesh and blood. The enemy wants us to see His negativity, but we must fight the good fight of faith.

Jeremiah 3:14 KJV

Return, O backsliding children says the Lord for I am married to you. I will take you from a city and two from a family, and I will bring you to Zion.

After so many years of wrestling with the enemy, we must become a candidate of faith. I had to realize after so many years that crying over what the enemy did to me was not moving the hand of God at all.

Yes, I must admit he sees our tears and knows our pain, but this does us not much good if we are not willing to go the extra mile. He is only happy when we exercise our faith in Him!

Above all, taking the shield of faith, wherewith ye may be able to quench all the fiery darts of the wicked.

Ephesians 6:16

We must always be willing to trust God in all situations of our life even when we are experiencing our darkest moments. Faith is that substance that strengthens us, and it is not late. It's a get-up right-now thing. Let me help to explain; when I used to read the verse referring to faith, to be honest, I never got the message right away. It wasn't until I had been beaten up by the enemy repeatedly that I then recognized that even the enemy knew I didn't understand the power of the verse.

But as soon as I understood this, faith took me to the next dimension of my life. I started to realise it's not a tomorrow faith, but God was telling me from this very moment to get up and fight back! You, too, might not have understood what the enemy was doing to you. Remember it is his intention that our vision stays blurred, however, we are wide awake and have been anointed to win.

Now faith is the substance of things hoped for, the evidence of things not seen.

Hebrews 11:1

Little did I know through all the fighting with the enemy God was calling me to become a good witness of His truth. Like me, I never realised that He has been maturing me to withstand the scheme of the enemy that blind and blurred.

Vision cannot be restored, if our sight is not restored back to us, we will be held captive as a prisoner forever. I had to realize that it was time to come out of my cage forever and that my hiding place had finally come to an end. You, too, might be saying it's your time, I'm convinced it is hot, read on!

Fight the good fight of faith, lay hold on eternal life whereunto thou art also called, and hast professed a good profession before many witnesses.

1Timothy 6:12

I now understand that after going through so much pain that God was preparing me for my task ahead. He knew that in order for me to win the race it must take a lot of training. I never understood at first that it would come with so much disappointment in so many areas of my life. Today I can truly admit that He knew just what He was permitting. If I was to become a skilled fighter He knew it would take that and much more. Looking back over my life I realized that all of my setbacks and delays were in the hands of God

After all, He know his plans towards me even when I didn't know them for myself. He was bigger than the pain I was feeling. He is bigger than your mistakes. He was always in it! Even when I thought he was not there, I came to understand that He knows our set time. Everything is in His hands. He is never late, although I often felt like I had missed my season. He had to remind me through His word that times and seasons are in His hands. He's the master of the ship and everything was only working for my good. Can I say it's working for your good? God always has a plan.

Luke 21:18

The spirit of the Lord is upon because the Lord hath anointed me: he hath sent me to preach good tidings unto the meek, he hath sent me to bind up the broken hearted to proclaim liberty to the captives, and the opening of the prison to them that are bound.

CHAPTER 10

The Will of God

Chapter Ten

After many years of dark nights, I realise that my will had to be aborted in order to receive God's will. It was not easy for me to accept what God wanted for me in the beginning, but if I was to become a skilled soldier in the race, I have to renew the will of God for my life in order to stay in the race

I must admit that after everything I've gone through inclusive of receiving the perfect will of God for my life that would have ended all of my tribulations, it was difficult to find out the fight had gotten even harder.

Saying, father, if thou be willing, remove this cup from me: nevertheless, not my will but thine will be done.

Luke 22:42

However, it was so important to me that I was in a much better position to fight. I was not alone, His grace was always there connecting to the trials and His strength was made perfect in my weakness. I have come to realise I was a better soldier because of many of the struggles that the enemy was using I was now able to recognise them.

His will was connecting to my pain, but the pain had produced a fire that, I will further explain. You must realise that early in any fight you never win all the time. Every time you lose you discover your weakness; after many years of experience or should I say after losing many fights you become more experience as to why you lose. This helps you to become a better fighter.

I have fought a good fight, I have kept the faith henceforth there is laid up for me a crown of righteousness, which the Lord, the righteous judge, shall give me at that day and not to me only, but unto all them also that love his appearing.

2 Timothy 4:7-8

You have been given a task, and you are not a quitter. You must win! My many disappointments, setbacks, frustration and delays have helped to produce a fire. I was able to withstand the test now. Each level takes me higher. Each height produces oil that is the anointing. No crushing, no oil! With every elevation, the fire of God shows up, but in order for that to occur, we need the oil. The oil or the fire of God can only come when we pass our test. We are never a good candidate to fight the enemy if we are not willing to suffer for the cause of righteousness.

When God has a plan for our life, though He causes grief He is still compassionate. I never understood it in the beginning, but I now understand if I'm to win, it takes all that I've gone through and more. I needed the fire that had been replaced by my pain. I really couldn't understand this fire. I was now in a place with God where every time the enemy came the fire of God showed up. Your pain can be replaced by the fire of God if you are willing and ready to climb heights.

1 Peter 3:14

But if ye suffer for righteousness sake, happy are ye: and be not afraid of their terror, neither be troubled.

I am here to say although all the odds were against me, I am now in a resting place and yes, I confess like the prophet Jeremiah I wanted at times to stay silent. It seems like when I mentioned or just talked about God's name, my opposer was always there.

Even though I wanted to be silent I had a wall of defence surrounding me. I am no longer afraid! I am a burning fire that cannot go out! I am now ready to pick a fight with the enemy whichever way he comes.

Then I said, I will not make mention of him, nor speak any more in his name. But his word was in mine heart as a burning fire shut up in my bones, and I could not stay.

Jeremiah 20:9 KJV

I am here to say nothing comes easy. After many years of being caged and discouraged God indeed had a plan. His ways are not our ways neither are His thoughts our thoughts. His goal is to bring us into His perfect will for our lives. He wanted us to win over the powers of darkness. He wanted us to be able to stand up to all the enemy's' schemes but so often we fail in believing He is able to do it. It took me many years. I was tricked by the devil' crafty schemes, but God is always a good God. Yes, He will never leave us, and neither will He forsake us.

We must be willing and ready to accept His will for our lives. No matter what, His thoughts towards us are good. Even when we don't understand the call, just answer. He is faith all by Himself, and I had to find out for myself that my tears and years of crying were not moving His hands toward me- instead, it was my willingness to say yes to His will and to His way. Faith moves Him, my friends. Don't hesitate to answer Him. He will guide you through every step of the way. Let's move on.

Isaiah 10:27

And it shall come to pass in that day, that his burden shall be taken away from off thy shoulder, and his yoke from off thy neck, and the yoke shall be destroyed because of the anointing.

Looking back over my life it was clear that God's plan and purpose for my life were to use me to help set the captive free from whatever spirits had them bound. His plan and purpose for my life are to help many that are suffering from the traps and snares and pitfalls of the enemy, to be set completely free and to open their eyes to the destructive plots and plans of the enemy.

In order for me to have been able to do this, I needed just what he gave me: a yoke-destroying anointing. It took many many years of suffering, but it was worth the fight. I am here to say, the enemy will never give up but when you have gone through the process you learn your techniques and strategies and are able to beat the enemy at his game.

And it shall come to pass in that day that his burden shall be taken away from off thy shoulder and his yoke from off your neck, and the yoke will be destroyed because of the anointing oil.

Isaiah 10:27

Rest assured that the enemy will never give up. His plan is to deceive us every step of the way. We must be alert at all times having on our full armour. We have been reminded of the word above, "All else taking the shield of faith which is able to quench all the fiery darts of hell's agents". Always remember that you're in it to win it! You cannot let down your guard. The enemy is constantly looking for open doors from our past. He is our accuser; he wants to remind God of all negativity. We must be smart to close all open doors.

One open door can cause you years of unnecessary fighting if you are not aware. I remember a time in my life that I was getting angry also. It seems as if it was out of control and I had many times questioned myself. Yes, I was doing my best to be a good Christian, but being a good Christian was not good enough. The door to anger had to be closed. Frustration had crept in and was letting down my guard. The enemy was winning. I address this because we fail to understand that it's the little things or the little foxes that spoil the vine.

2 Corinthians 11:14

And no marvel; for Satan himself is transformed into an angel of light.

The enemy is always aware of opening doors. He doesn't care who you are, or where you come from. His goal is to bring accusations against you. You must always seek to try your very best to keep closed doors shut. You will be happy when you do.

God wants us to be blessed in every area of our lives. Many of us are not living to our very full potential because we refuse to close doors. Some of these doors are anger, hatred, strife, backbiting etc. Walking in the perfect will of God for our lives calls for all open doors to be shut which will cause the blessings of God to cease.

And I heard a lower voice saying in heaven, now is come salvation and strength, and the kingdom of our good and the power of his Christ; For the accuser of our brethren is cast down, which accused them before God day and night.

Revelations 12:10

God wants us to walk in total victory over all the works of the flesh. He reminds us in His words that to be carnally minded is death. He wants us to live a fulfilled life of long-term happiness, but it's our choice. I choose life and am confident that you will choose life also! We must never forget that this race is from time to eternity.

But if you are a skilled candidate you will always survive the enemy's schemes. I cannot tell you that you won't fail. At times, I did, multiple times. However, I quickly recognized the scheme. After all, I've been trained for this and don't despair you will too.

Galatians 5: 19-21

19. Now the works of the flesh are manifest, which are these, adultery, fornication, uncleanness, lasciviousness.

20. Idolatry, witchcraft, hatred, variance, emulations, wrath, strife, seditions, heresies.

21. Envying, murders, drunkness, revellings and such like: of which I tell you before as I have also told you in time past, that they which do such things shall not inherit the kingdom of God.

CHAPTER 11

Never Say 'I Can't'

Chapter Eleven

The enemy loves to hear you say the words, "I can't". This is one of the main tools he uses: our mind. Your mind is your battleground. The victory is either won or lost in the mind. Your mind is connected to your body, spirit and soul. Once the enemy has your mind he has full control of you. I have been placed under mind control for many years. I'm addressing this because this is if not, the most powerful weapon that the enemy uses among many believers today. Once your mind is under control your head malfunctions. You cannot reason or think clearly. The enemy knows that once this stronghold has been placed over you his job becomes easy for the spirit of deception to move in.

Note that the enemy's job is to bring separation between you and God. He likes and delights in stagnation. Of course, he finds joy in going to our Father with accusations. With a malfunctioning mind, he is able to deceive us every step of the way. His job is to take you back to the cage he once had you in. If you like me have ever had a real cage experience, you won't want to go back. You will love your new freedom. Your mind is clear. The enemy knows if he cannot deceive you, his plans have been cancelled.

Philippians 4:13

I can do all things through Christ who strengthens me.

Our Father knows his plan, He promised us that every evil work will be brought into judgement. No matter what the enemy is plotting it has already been cancelled by the blood of Jesus. His purpose for dying on the cross was to destroy the works of the devil.

We have been given the authority by our Lord and Saviour, Jesus Christ to destroy his works. He can never win over a true child of God. We must never be discouraged. Our goal is to always be ahead of the game.

He that committeth sin is of the devil, for the devil sinneth from the beginning: for this purpose the son of God was manifested that he might destroy the works of the devil.

1 John 3:8

We have been given authority over all the powers of darkness. Our Lord had fought hell and he won! Today we can claim victory in every situation, Satan knows that he has forever lost his place in the kingdom of God and his intention is to stop you and me from this once-in-a-lifetime opportunity. But we have been given the power to tread upon him, God had allowed us to see and understand his dark side so that we can overcome it!

After having so many fights with the enemy I realize that Satan and his agents know you and for many of us, we sometimes feel as if this is a plus. I must admit I did too, but I have come to learn that it was not so much the spirits becoming subject to you, but that I had to endeavour to keep the unity with both God and men.

Luke 18:19

18. And he said unto them, I beheld Satan as lightning fall from heaven.

19. Behold I give unto you power to tread on serpents and scorpions, and over all the power of the enemy: and nothing shall by any means hurt you.

Today I can say my goal is to make heaven my future home after years of toil on this side of Planet Earth. I am working for a home not built with men's hands but eternal in the kingdom of heaven.

In conclusion to the matter, rejoice not because the spirits are subject to you, but rejoice because you made heaven your choice!

Notwithstanding in this rejoice not, that the spirits are subject unto you, but rather rejoice because your names are written in heaven.

Luke 10:20

Letters To God

Letters
To God

Letters
To God

Letters
To God

Letters
To God

Letters
To God

Letters To God

Letters
To God

Letters
To God

Letters
To God

Letters
To God

ABOUT

THE AUTHOR

Apostle Rosemary Duncanson is a unique and rare vessel to the body of Christ. She is a mother, Pastor and Teacher. Having proclaimed the Word of God for more than three decades, her yoke-broking anointing has helped many across all spheres of life. Apostle Dunacanson enjoys her outreach ministries and reaches out to as many as possible, calling darkness into light. After many years of pain, hurt and disappointments she is making full proof of her ministries, and is determined that the enemy will not win. Her determination has given her recognition in every area of her life.

Printed in the USA
CPSIA information can be obtained
at www.ICGtesting.com
LVHW021548301023
762206LV00003B/47